Heuch

*Aileen S*ı

Front cover: leaf of *Heuchera* **'Oakington Jewel',** introduced in 1935 by Alan Bloom, who is President of the Hardy Plant Society, and was named after his first nursery at Oakington, near Cambridge.

Illustrations by:
Sally Grant, Gwen Grantham, Jean Rush

Edited and typeset by George Parker
Consultant editor to the Booklet Series: Tony Lord

©The Hardy Plant Society - May 2004
ISBN 0 901687 21 9

Heuchera 'Rachel'

Acknowledgements

I would like to thank the following people for their help and support in providing information: Bob Brown (Cotswold Garden Flowers), Dan Heims (Terra Nova Nurseries Inc., USA), Luc Klinkhamer, Charles and Martha Oliver (Primrose Path Nurseries), the Rancho Santa Ana Botanic Garden USA, the New York Botanical Garden, the Royal Horticultural Society, the Santa Rosa Botanical Garden, the United States Department of Agriculture. I also would like to acknowledge the use that I have made of the Jepson Manual of Higher Plants of California.

Johann Heinrich von Heucher

3

Introduction

ORIGINALLY CLASSIFIED BY CARL LINNAEUS in 1753 this genus was named after Johann Heinrich von Heucher (1677-1747) who was a notable Professor of both Medicine and Botany at the University of Wittenberg in Germany and later at Dresden. He was also Physician-in-Ordinary to Augustus II of Poland. It was customary for plants to be named after famous people and there was a Botanic Garden at Wittenberg so it was probable that Heucher was familiar with the plant that bears his name, particularly as botany and medicine went hand in hand, for healing relied heavily on plant material then, as it does now.

This genus is native to North America, chiefly in the west, ranging from British Columbia in the north to Mexico in the south, the notable exception being *H. americana* for this is native to the eastern side of the USA. There are many different species listed in the Kew Botanical Gardens' archives alone and probably more elsewhere but nearly all are native to the states close to the Rocky Mountains. The states where they are indigenous such as Wyoming, Colorado, Ohio, Oregon, Nevada, Idaho and New Mexico, for instance, conjure up a mental picture of the 'Indian Country' associated with the American Indians. It is not surprising, therefore, to learn that almost every species has the word 'alum' attached to its common name, indicating that it was, and still is in some cases, an important source of this substance.

Alum is very soluble in water, is extracted from the root and is a powerful astringent. Introduced to medicine by the American Indians it is still used to reduce inflammation of the mucus membranes and to curtail passive bleeding, and it is known to be active against various strains of *Mycobacterium tuberculosis*. It is also an excellent mordant for the dyeing of wool. The roots of heucheras are rich in tannin – a vital ingredient for the tanning of animal skin so this genus would have played an important part in the life of both the native population and the 'settlers'.

Sadly, many of the species are threatened in their native areas by extensive lumbering. The felling of large tracts of forest for wood and increasingly for development and extensive recreational purposes has resulted in the loss of the ground cover and many species are now on the danger list. Environmental bodies in the States affected are aware of this and are struggling to protect as many as possible.

As with other members of the *Saxifragaceae* family, species in the genus *Heuchera* share the common characteristics. They form basal rosettes of leaves from which rise stiff stems of flowers with sprays of tiny blooms. The leaves are usually green with some red in either stem or vein and the flowers range from white through pink to red. They are shallow rooted and prefer dappled shade but most will tolerate less than perfect conditions. Ideally, they will thrive and give of their best in humus rich soil with good drainage, but do not like drought. There are some heucheras in this book that have not reached the UK yet so it is difficult to ascertain their degree of hardiness. Hardiness Zones are only given for the species, and other conditions have to be considered such as soil, pH, situation and drainage; the latter is important for heucheras as they are not their happiest in heavy clay. The only advice about these newcomers 'fresh from the crèche' so to speak, is to check the parentage where possible, as this will give some clues, or to 'take a chance'. After all, even the most expensive will not break the budget. They make good garden plants and can be used in a variety of situations. As a rule, heucheras behave themselves as they remain compact, so do not intrude on other plants' territory. Some make good groundcover but as they are not particularly good spreaders need to be planted in larger quantities. Although the flowers have a quiet charm, most have a relatively short flowering period in late spring and early summer and the major value of the plants is the foliage. The leaves, especially of the more recent introductions, are a kaleidoscope of colour and shape and quite often persistent in the winter, giving year round value to the gardener.

The early breeding was concentrated on improvement of the flowers both in size and range of colour. In the 1930s many heucheras were immensely popular as cut flowers; there was a flourishing commercial trade and it was largely for this reason that Blooms raised so many cultivars. Recently the emphasis has been on leaf shape, texture and colour.

In the nineteenth century Lemoine focused on breeding for improved flowers and used the name *H. x brizoides* for those cultivars resulting from crossing *H. americana* and *H. sanguinea*. However, since then, other species have been introduced, *H. micrantha* for instance, and the parentage of many of the named varieties has been lost. The Bloom family, from Bressingham in Norfolk, have also given us some lovely cultivars; the cultivars named after the planets came from Aart Wijhnoux in the Netherlands, but the recent 'explosion' has emanated from the USA. Concentrated breeding programmes by Dan Heims, Charles and Martha Oliver, and others, have transformed the wide spectrum of leaf colour. Coupled with this has been a tremendous advance in variations of leaf shape and size so that there is surely now a heuchera for any garden or colour scheme whether it be for foliage or flower.

As the foliage remains low, the best situations are obviously at the front of flower borders and lovely ribbon effects can be achieved by using the same cultivar along the edge; a careful choice can give a permanent structure all the year. If planted for the flowers the best results are with group rather than dot planting as this gives the maximum effect when in bloom. They are also a great asset to containers and will do well in these conditions. Some of the species grow naturally in the mesic forests. Here the conditions are neither very wet nor very dry throughout the year. These forests are dominated by a canopy of sugar maples, beech and yellow birch, with a few conifers. Soils are rich and can sustain a wide diversity of plant species. Thus, good combinations can be achieved by using heucheras in similar places in the garden, as under-planting in airy shrub borders and rose beds or as permanent planting amongst annual bedding. Obviously, as many of them are happy in light woodland conditions, they will mingle quite well here with our own native plants as they are not intrusive in character. There seems to be a leaf or flower colour to complement any or all planting schemes.

In an earlier booklet in this series, *Saxifragaceae* published 1995, the heucheras were only given a chapter and the cultivars/varieties/selections were listed under their parent species, as is the case in *The RHS Plant Finder*, with a short list of the new cultivars at the end. However, as there are now so many cultivars, for easy reference for the reader the species are listed first and the cultivars in alphabetical order follow separately. Hopefully, this will be advantageous for the practical use of the book for reference purposes. The parentage, where known, has been given in abbreviated form with each entry.

No attempt has been made to describe all the species – only those pertinent to the subject of breeding programmes, garden plants and presently available on the market.

During my research I found that there are some discrepancies in the descriptions of these plants; these could be for various reasons: climate, soil, position and personal ideas of colour and form can all contribute to apparent differences in the growth of any plant and heucheras are no exception. Added to these is the consideration that for some of the older cultivars, selective breeding, whether accidental or conscious, will, over time, result in conflicting descriptions.

Cultivation & Propagation

THE MAJORITY OF HEUCHERA CULTIVARS are bred from species native to the light woodland areas of North America and, bearing this in mind, it would be sensible to give similar conditions in garden situations. Most are easy and will tolerate a fairly wide variety of soil, sun and shade but, being shallow rooted, will perform better in a moist, humus rich soil in dappled shade. They do not like to be waterlogged nor subjected to prolonged periods of drought. Purple-leaved varieties respond to a little more sun or they will stay green. In the recent trials at Wisley, the darkest leaves scorched in sunshine after showers, from late spring into early summer; sometimes this can kill off the flowering shoots. Bright sun can make the purple/red colouration more intense and can add deeper tones to the yellow sorts such as 'Amber Waves'. Removal of flowering stems will induce better leaf production but this is anathema to some gardeners.

Propagation can be by division in early autumn, staunchly advocated by Alan Bloom, or in spring in the north and west of the UK. The plants tend to push themselves out of the ground in winter, especially the older crowns, and can benefit from division every two or three years. Either re-plant deeper or pull off the woody stems and plant the younger pieces. Seed from the species can be sown, as fresh as possible, and will come true provided it has not been fertilized by another species or cultivar. Seed from cultivars will not necessarily resemble the parent but may result in a nice surprise! The seed is very fine and needs to be sown thinly, left uncovered, and watered carefully - preferably mist sprayed. Germination is not good and can take up to 90 days at a temperature of 16°-21°.

At a recent (2004) HPS Study Day on heucheras the main speaker, Rosie Hardy of Hardy's Cottage Garden Plants, who is passionate about this genus, gave some excellent advice on cultivation. She advocates a good tidy up in the spring, removing old winter foliage and cutting back hard any old woody stems. She assures that within three to four weeks new growth will appear. To encourage heucheras to repeat flower, do not cut off faded flower stalks but slide fingers down the stalk to a few inches above attachment and pull off with a slight twist in order to leave a small heel on the stem. This injury to the plant will usually stimulate further flower production.

Most heucheras need twelve weeks of vernalization to flower. This issue of vernalization probably does not arise in the UK. Many of the heucheras are grown in warmer climes in North America and will not have the extremes of temperature experienced in the UK and consequently might not be so floriferous. Thus, if one chooses a variety based on the flower rather that the foliage it is advisable to ensure that it receives a cold spell in the year, as is usual in winter in most places in the UK.

Some of the cultivars are seed raised and developed as true-breeding maintenances. Some are reproduced by tissue culture and Dr. Lord found that, particularly when the plants are young, they can be very unlike the originals, though some of them do seem to settle down after a while. Characteristics can vary considerably as the result of tissue culture. Some nurseries will use their own seed to raise plants that will not necessarily be the true form but in practice it can be difficult to identify accurately a specific variety at the point of purchase.

Some of the plants in this booklet are protected by patent and it is illegal to propagate these without permission from the breeder. The abbreviations referring to these are given at the beginning of the section on cultivars, page 17.

Hardiness Zones

Zone	Average Minimum Winter Temperature	
3	-40 to -34°C	(-40 to -30°F)
4	-34 to -29°C	(-30 to -20°F)
5	-29 to -23°C	(-20 to -10°F)
6	-23 to -18°C	(-10 to 0°F)
7	-18 to -12° C	(0 to 10°F)
8	-12 to -7°C	(10 to 20°F)
9	-7 to -1° C	(20 to 30°F)
10	-1 to 4°C	(30 to 40°F)
11	above 4° C	(40 to 50°F)

Pests & Diseases

ALTHOUGH THE GENUS *HEUCHERA* is relatively free from pests and disease, plants can succumb to the following:

Anthracnose - This fungal disease causes small brown spots.

Botrytis cinerea (grey mould) - This causes large, brown spots and/or a grey mould.

Corynebacterium fascians syn *Rhodococcus fascians* (leafy gall). This phyto-pathogenic bacterium provokes shoot meristem formation and malformations on aerial plant parts, mainly at the axils. It is advisable to destroy the plants if infection occurs. It lives in the soil and the exact means of infection is uncertain – in some cases it is transmitted by seed. Destroy the affected plants and do not replant with susceptible species for as long as possible.

Pseudomonas – This bacterium causes reddish brown spots that may cause the leaf to distort

Xanthomonas - This bacterium causes small, brown, angular to circular spots with yellow halos.

The aforementioned diseases should not be confused with irregular, bleached, dead areas on the leaves that are due to over exposure to excessive hot sun.

There are various commercial products for the treatment of these diseases but good hygiene, improved ventilation if indoors, regular inspection and immediate removal and destruction of affected plant material will help maintain good health and better resistance to these conditions.

When conditions are excessively unfavourable heucheras can be affected by powdery mildew and, of course, the dreaded vine weevil, *Otiorhynchus sulcatus*, to which heucheras are particularly susceptible.

The adult weevil is black, measures 10-12mm long, and hides in the top layers of soil, be it in a container or open ground. They start to feed in May and lay eggs about four weeks later through to late September. The eggs are laid around the host plant root system and when hatched, the larvae feed on the roots. The adults emerge and feed on the foliage; they are slow moving and easily seen indoors near houseplants in early summer. Early signs of infestation include irregular shaped notches where the leaves have been eaten by adults, plants showing stress and separated from their roots by the feeding larvae.

Prophylaxis is the best weapon against this now ubiquitous pest. All plants should be inspected carefully, especially the roots if pot grown, before introducing to the garden. There are now many commercial products on the market to curtail this unwanted guest.

Good biological control can be by nematodes such as *Steinernema carpocapsae* and *Heterorhabditis megidis*

The following website gives information on legal pesticides in the U.K: http://www.pesticides.gov.uk

For the USA go to: http://www.epa.gov/pesticides

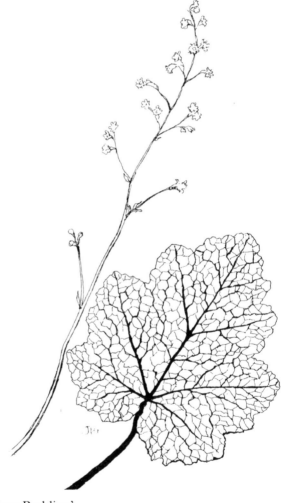

Heuchera 'Plum Pudding'

Heuchera species

Heuchera abramsii (syn. *H. rubescens* var. *abramsii*) San Gabriel Alumroot, Abrams' Alumroot
This is a native of the USA, especially of California, found in dry rocky areas up to 3,500 metres (11,483ft) high. It is similar to *H. alpestris* with deeply lobed leaves 5-15mm wide and white flowers in spring. It grows from 5-15cm (2-6in) high and likes a cool, shady spot with humus rich soil. Sow seed in spring on surface or divide in spring. A good choice for the alpine house.

H. americana (*H. lucida, H. glauca*), American Alumroot (rock geranium, satin leaf). Z 4 -10
Native to much of eastern North America and in cultivation since 1656, this species is mainly grown for its decorative, 15-20cm (6-8in) high foliage, which is tough, leathery and lobed, dark green in colour and copper-veined when young. As the leaves persist it can be useful for the winter garden and it forms good groundcover. The greenish-white flowers appear in the late spring. This has probably had the greatest influence on the recent cultivar introductions that have concentrated on foliage, especially the emphasis on the silvery and metallic effects. As a parent of a cultivar it often gives a line of colour along the leaf edge, as in *H.* 'Ring of Fire', with its red edge, and *H.* 'Coral Bouquet', where the edge is yellow.

_H.a._ 'Purpurea' A name sometimes misapplied to *H. rubescens*.
Similar to the species but the undersides of the leaves are marbled brown and the flowers are white.

H. bracteata Rocky Mountain Alumroot
This is a native in the west of North America, in rocky areas of Colorado and Wyoming. The leaves are orbiculate and shallowly lobate with spinose teeth. The flowers in the panicle are small and dense 3-15cm (1-6in) high, blooming in summer. The leaves are bronze-green. It prefers rock crevices but not too dry with some shade in summer.
Sow seed in spring, or divide in spring. Take root cuttings in the autumn.

H. brevistaminea Laguna Mountain Alumroot
A native of SW USA. on the dry, rocky slopes of California between 1,500 and 2,000m (4,920 and 6560ft). The orbiculate, shallowly lobed leaves are shallowly dentate and white ciliate. The petiole is white and hirsute. The red-purple flowers are in a narrow, lax panicle 15-30cm (6-12in) high. It prefers a sunny, dry site and protection from winter wet.

Sow seed or divide in spring or take root cuttings in the autumn.

H. x *brizoides* Hort. Ex Lemoine Z4 -10

These are hybrids of *H. sanguinea* and *H. americana*, and possibly also *H. micrantha*. Raised in France in the late-nineteenth century, they will grow in sun or light shade, are hardy and usually free-flowering. The name was originally used for plants with small flowers on slender stems, such as 'Gracillima'

H. cespitosa (syn. *H. rubescens* var. *cespitosa*) Tufted Alumroot

This is native to California - and is closely related to *H. rubescens*. A late spring bloomer it is to be found in rock crevices but needs both a good water supply and good drainage.

H. cylindrica Round Leaf Alumroot. Z4

A native of Nevada, Wyoming, and Montana, west to California and British Columbia. The kidney-shaped leaves are wider than they are long. In its natural state it is found on cliffs and rocks. It prefers a well-drained soil. Cylindrical spike-like inflorescences of cream or green flowers 15-90cm (6-36in) high appear in spring through to late summer, but it is usually planted for the foliage. The wavy-edged leaves form dark green mats.

H.c. 'Alba'

Similar to the species with cream flowers.

H.c. var. *alpina*

This variety has flowers creamy-white to green, sometimes tipped with pink, in spike-like inflorescences 8.5 to 55cm (3½-21in) tall, with pubescent foliage. It differs from *H. cylindrica* in having larger leaves and petioles glandular to stiff-hairy.

H. duranii Hard Alumroot

A native of California and Nevada in the SW of the USA and found on the rocky slopes. The basal leaves are kidney/round in shape and shallowly crenate, the plant having a tuft-like shape. The flowers are 15-35cm (6-14in) high and yellow and pink and appear in the spring. It prefers shade in summer and an adequate water supply.

H. elegans syn. *H. hirsuta* – *H. rubescens* var. *elegans* Urn-flowered Alumroot

Native of the San Gabriel Mountains of California, 1,500-2,000m (4,920 and 6560ft), it has shallowly lobate leaves and the petiole is hirsute. Blooming in late spring it needs protection from winter wet and a sunny, dry position. Its growth is tuft like and reaches about 25 cm (10in) in height.

H. glabra Alpine Heuchera. Z4
A native of Oregon to Alaska, this stoloniferous species has rounded or heart-shaped, deeply lobed leaves that colour in the autumn. It makes good groundcover. Its conspicuous white flowers are 50cm (20in) tall in early summer.

H. glauca see *H. americana*

H. grossulariifolia (syn. *H. cusickii*) Gooseberry Leaf Alumroot. Z5
A native of Oregon, Montana, Washington and Idaho, USA, this was named in 1900. It is very free flowering and showy, having pure white, bell flowers and a height of 10-50cm (4-20in). It gets its name from the shape of the leaves that resemble those of the gooseberry plant, being cordate-orbiculate with 5-7 lobes. Needs protection from winter wet. Sow seed in spring or take root cuttings in the autumn.

H. hallii Front Range Alumroot. Z3
Originally from Pikes Peak, Colorado, this is one of the most delicate heucheras with slender 20cm (8in) spikes of white bells in the spring over clumps of small, toothed leaves. It is a shade lover, forms a tuft, and is a high altitude plant.

H. hirsutissima Shaggyhair Alumroot. Z 6 -9
A native of the thickets in California and San Jacinto Mountains 2,200-3,500m (7,200-11,483ft), it resembles *H. elegans* and likes a moist, rich soil and a sunny aspect with good drainage. Blooms in summer. 25cm (10in) high.

H. hispida see *H. pilosissima*

H. longiflora (syn. *H. aceroides*) Long Flower Alumroot
Native to the grasslands of SE USA. The leaves are orbiculate, cordate, and 5/7 lobate with acute teeth. The large flowers are yellow and purple and form a conical panicle 60-80cm (24-30in) high in summer. It likes good loam and a sunny site.

H. macrophylla
This is 60cm (2ft) high with bronze foliage. Possibly this species does not exist any more, as it has not appeared in recent publications.

H. maritima
This is not a validated name. It was grown from seed by W.E.Th. Ingwersen Ltd. but did not prove to be of any great interest.

H. maxima Jill o' the Rocks. Z6 -10
Found only on cliffs in canyons above 500m (1,640ft) in the Californian Channel Islands, this is not quite so hardy as some species, growing to 60cm (2ft) with white, pink-tinged flowers and bright green leaves.

H. merriamii Merriam's Alumroot. Z7
A low spreading alpine, from the rocky slopes of California and Oregon, with pink flowers to about 20cm. (8in) high in late spring, forming a cushion.

H. mexicana
Delicate sprays of white flowers on dark stems open from pink buds from April until June.

H. micrantha Crevice Alumroot. Z5 -9
A native of western North America, this species has conspicuously attractive grey-marbled leaves and many white flowers with red to orange anthers on stems up to 90cm (3ft) high. Blooming in early summer, the seed usually comes true.

H.m. var. **diversifolia**
Found in Vancouver Island in British Columbia and in Washington, it flowers from spring to early summer. The leaves are interesting; they are nearly round in the winter but lobed in the summer.

H. parishii Mill Creek Alumroot
This Californian species is similar to *H. rubescens* and is possibly of hybrid origin, involving *H. hirsutissima* and *H. rubescens*. Smaller plants from higher elevations have been called *H. alpestris* but this is not a synonym of the species as a whole. The leaves, 15-40mm (½-1½in) wide, form a cushion. The narrow flower panicle is 10-30cm (4-12in) high in late spring. It prefers a sunny, dry position with protection from winter wet.

H. parviflora Little Flower Alumroot
Native of eastern USA

H. parvifolia Little Leaf Alumroot. Z5
This is a native of the Rocky Mountains, from New Mexico to Montana. Cream to white flower spikes in the summer grow to 38cm (15in) with round to kidney shaped leaves up to 6cm (2½in) wide. It is a high altitude, tuft-forming plant that likes a sunny position and protection from winter wet.

H. pilosissima (*H. hispida*) Seaside Alumroot. Z6 - 10
A native of California and Oregon, it grows in the coastal pine and redwood forests below 500m (1,640ft). It prefers cool, well-drained soil in partial shade. The leaves and stems are hairy, the stems, up to 55cm (22in), are brown and bear compact racemes of flowers with pinkish-white petals
There is another form of *H. pilosissima* that has white, velvety hairs and grey-pink flowers but it is not considered to be reliably hardy.

H. pringlei
This species is considered to be close to *H. merriamii*, though possibly of hybrid origin.

H. procrantzii
Once thought to be of mid-European origin, this is probably a hybrid. It has very small flowers that create a gypsophila-like effect in the border.

H. x pruhoniciana
Of hybrid origin, with parentage *H. cylindrica* and *H. sanguinea*, this is named after the Pruhonice Park near Prague. The compact pink flowers, turning to red, rise 50cm (20in) above the persistent leafy cushion base.

H. pubescens Downy Alumroot. Z5- 9
A native of central-eastern USA, this species grows to 75cm (2½ft), with bronze young leaves that colour well in the autumn. The flowers are greenish-white with purple markings.

H.p. 'Alba'
Similar to the species but with plain white flowers.

H. pulchella Sandia Mountain Alum Root. Z9
From New Mexico, this plant has a very thick rootstock. The margins of the bright green leaves have broad bristle-tipped teeth. Flowers purple to pink.

H. richardsonii Richardson's Alumroot. Z5
A native of British Colombia to Colorado and east to Indiana and Minnesota, the flowers are white with purple veins and the foliage is a rich reddish-brown. It grows 60-120cm (2-4ft) high. This plant was favoured by Gertrude Jekyll but whether this was the *H.richardsonii* in the National Collection (described as short-stemmed, with heart-shaped leaves with velvety white down and white flowers) is debateable. Older sources give *H. richardsonii* as a synonym of *H. hispida* and *H. americana*. No doubt the taxonomists will one day clarify this confusion.

H. rubescens Pink Alum Root
A native of northern California, Nevada and Utah. A good plant for the autumn: the leaves are an old-rose colour, turning copper and dark purple and crimson. The flowers are greeny-buff on short sprays, 10-30cm (4-12in) high. It has a tuft-like form of growth.

H.r. var. versicolor
Pink flowers from June to September.

H.r. Dwarf
Seed collected at Carson Pass, south of Lake Tahoe, California, at 2,591m (8,500 ft). A very small plant only reaching 5cm (2in) with pink flowers in May and June.

H.r. micans
This is not a validated name. A heavy blooming miniature with small leaves 2cm (1in) across, being a very neat plant. The short red stems bear wine-red panicles of white-tinged flowers 15cm (6in) high.

H. sanguinea Coral Bells. Z3 -9
This species has been in Britain since the middle of the nineteenth century and has remained quietly popular. In its native habitats, southern Arizona and north Mexico, it is found among moist, shady rocks. It will thrive in most conditions whether in sun or partial shade in cooler climates. The dark green leaves form low mats, showing off the bright coral-red flowers, 25-50cm (10-20in) high, from spring to autumn. It is a parent of many cultivars, particularly in the hybrid group *H. x brizoides.*

H.s. 'Alba' AGM
1896. Similar to the species but having plain, white flowers early in the season 30cm (1ft) high. The foliage is green and good in the winter.

H. villosa Hairy Alumroot. Z6
Comes from the mountains of eastern North America. It prefers well-drained leafy soil in partial shade but will tolerate deep shade and drought. Late to bloom, the loose panicles of pinkish-white flower are borne 40-60cm (16-24in) high. The huge hirsute leaves are maple-like in shape and often colour well in the autumn.

H.v. 'Purpurea'
This has purple satin-like leaves, darker than 'Palace Purple' with more bronze colouring. The white blooms appear in late summer. It is an easy plant and can make a good edging. It contrasts well with 'Autumn Bride', also a villosa, but having light green leaves.

H. 'Mint Frost'

Heuchera cultivars

ABBREVIATIONS USED IN THIS SECTION

<u>For heuchera species</u> :-
a	*americana*	*r*	*rubescens*
briz	x *brizoides*	*s*	*sanguinea*
cyl	*cylindrica*	*vill*	*villosa*
eleg	*elegans*		<u>Other abbreviations</u>:-
glab	*glabra*	V	variegated
glauc	*glauca*	var	botanical variety
max	*maxima*	AGM	Award of Garden Merit
merr	*merriamii*	EU	European Plant Variety Rights
m	*micrantha*	PP	US Plant Patent
pring	*pringlei*	PPAF	US Plant Patent Applied For
pub	*pubescens*	PVR	European Plant Variety Rights Applied For

Please note: The parentage of the cultivars, where known, is given after the name. Where only one parent is given this is believed to be the dominant parent.

Generally these flourish in Zones 5 - 10

'Adriana'
Has red flowers to 60cm (2ft) in May and June, above green leaves.

'Amber Waves'
D. Heims. (PP & EU). This has unique coloured leaves of yellow and amber topped by 30cm (1ft) stems of pink flowers in late spring and early summer. Voted best new plant for 2001.

'Amethyst Myst' (*m* x *a*)
D. Heims, 1996. A veil of silver spreads over the amethyst foliage of this plant and the glossy leaves can make clumps 60cm(2ft) across. A good foliage feature, with small, white flowers.

'Angel's Pink'
Named for Angel Guerzon, a Santa Cruz garden designer. Blooming in May and June this has pink flowers on 40cm (16in) stems above green leaves.

'Annemarie'
Pink flowers up to 35cm (14in) from May to July above green leaves.

'Apple Blossom' (*s*) A. Bloom, 1932. The 60cm (2ft) high, large, red-rimmed white flowers appear pink, in May until July and the leaves are green.

'Autumn Bride' (*vill*) (May sometimes appear as *H. villosa* var. *macrorrhiza*)

This seed-raised plant has a good drought tolerance and performs better than most heucheras in hot humid conditions. It shares the same characteristics as the species, with fuzzy, light green leaves, growing to 90cm (3ft) high with white to pinkish flowers in late summer. Good for ground cover at the base of trees.

'Autumn Haze'
D. Heims. (PP & EU). The foliage is cinnamon with a purple haze and strong veining. The rose-tinted flowers are 60cm (2ft) high in April through to September. This plant will respond well in sun and partial shade but needs good drainage.

'Barbara' (v)
The leaves are variegated, with cream, pink, and khaki-green colouring but the flowers are poor.

'Barbara's Findling' (v)
Cream, sectorial, cream speckled foliage with a grey overlay contrasts with the 25cm (10in) high, red flowers, in May and June.

'Bartram' (*m* x *a*)
Greenish/white flowers with a red tinge, 35cm (14in) high in late spring, over dark green leaves with dark red veins and silver markings. The leaves are 8-13cm (3-8in) wide and it will repeat flower in cooler situations. Makes a good edging plant or ground cover.

'Beauty'
Cream flowers 40cm (16in) high over brownish leaves in May and June.

'Beauty Colour'
The leaves are full of shades of red, edged silvery-white and deep purple, with pointed edges. The blooms, up to 50cm (20in) high appear in June and July. A lively looking, beautiful plant.

'Beldex'
Pink flowers 50cm (20in) high, over green leaves, in May and June.

'Benzi'
White flowers 60cm (2ft) high, over brown foliage, in May and June.

'Biddulph Brown' (*vill*)
Like the species it is later flowering but with brownish/red glossy foliage and many small white flowers on dark stems forming a columnar shape 50cm (20in) high from August to October. An easy plant.

Heuchera 'Beauty Colour'

'Black Beauty' see 'Dark Beauty'

X **'Blackbird'** AGM
The 30cm (1ft) high, creamy white flowers in early summer show well
against the rich, dark brown of the ruffled leaves.

'Blood Vein' (*a*)
This is a selected form of *H. americana* with the usual thick, rounded
and lobed leaves, but brightly decorated with deep crimson veins and
producing sprays of greenish/pink flowers.

'Brandon Pink' (*s*) (*v*)
A hardy selection with bright, coral pink flowers growing to 60cm (2ft)
and green and white foliage.

'Bressingham Blaze' (*s*)
A. Bloom, 1950. Sprays of fiery red, large, open bellflowers, 60cm (2ft)
high are borne in spring over marbled leaves.

Bressingham Bronze ('Absi') (*H. m.* var. *d.*)
A. Bloom. This cultivar is distinct from 'Palace Purple' and has been
vegetatively raised. It has large, bronze-purple, crinkled leaves that are
bright purple beneath and arching stems of fine, off-white flowers 60cm
(2ft) high. It blooms from late spring to late summer.

'Bronze Beacon' (syn 'Red on Bronze')
A very good plant having bronze/green foliage, ruffled, and deep purple
on the undersides. The light pink flowers bloom from April until June
and are good. It is vigorous but with a dense habit. In the RHS trials of
1996-98 it received full marks for its foliage.

'Bronze Wave' (*villosa*)
C. Oliver, 1998. This dark leaved, large heuchera has wavy margins to
the hairy leaves that can reach 15-20cm (6-8in) across. It makes a
clump up to 60cm (2ft) across and bears wands of pinkish white flowers
in mid to late summer.

'Brown Coral' (x *pruhoniciana*)
Tight, upright spikes of brown/coral flowers in May until July and later.
A compact and easy plant.

X **'Burgundy Frost'** AGM for foliage in 2000
D. Heims, 1986. This was imported by the HPS and took part in the
Wisley Trials. Cream flowers 20/50cm (8-20in) high appear in May and
June, above silvery-purple leaves with dark veins and maroon
underneath. It has a frosted appearance and good leaf shape but was
superseded by 'Can-can'.

✗ 'Can-can' (*m* x *a*) AGM.

D. Heims, 1996. This is the first of the 'ruffles' to take on the metallic silvers forming a tight, ruffled mound. The flowers are pale green. It was awarded a gold medal in Belgium.

The Canyon Quartet Series were bred by Dara Emery in 1993 and released by Santa Barbara Botanic Garden after his death. There are also others in the 'Canyon' collection. They form small, mat-like plants with round, green leaves that are good ground cover

'Canyon Belle'

D. Emery. (PP). Dainty and shorter, with red flowers.

'Canyon Chimes'

D. Emery. (PP). A hybrid from H. elegans and 'Canyon Delight'. A taller variety bearing dark fuchsia-red flowers over a long period and preferring light shade and partial sun. The leaves are evergreen and it can form good groundcover.

'Canyon Duet'

D. Emery. (PP). This is a small plant with bi-coloured flowers of pink and white.

'Canyon Melody'

D. Emery, 2001. (PP). A small plant with pink and white petalled flowers. It is a diminutive form of one of its parents, being a hybrid of 'Canyon Pink' and *H. elegans*. The 30cm (1ft) high flowers are borne on dark stems above bright green leaves that resemble those of London Pride. The persistent leaves are mat forming.

'Canyon Blushing Bells'

D. Emery. Forms loose mats of dark green leaves and 30cm (1ft) high stems of off-white to pale pink flowers. Low growing.

'Canyon Delight' (*eleg* x *s*)

D. Emery, 1985. Outstanding plant with dense masses of deep green foliage with stiff panicles of dark pink flowers. Makes good low-growing ground cover.

'Canyon Pink' (*eleg* x *s*)

D. Emery, 1985. A very compact plant, the foliage is only 8cm (3in) tall and 30cm (1ft) wide. It has good sprays of very deep pink flowers. In the RHS trials of 1996-98 it received high marks for the green foliage.

'Capuccino' (*m* x *a*)

D. Heims, 1996. The colour of the leaves is creamy-coffee and being sun-resistant it mingles well with gold and yellow plants and flowers.

'Carmen' (*s*)
A. Bloom, 1950. Intense carmine-pink, medium sized flowers 60cm (2ft) high appear in the spring. The leaves are dark green and it is recommended.

'Carousel' (*m* x *a*)
Rosy red flowers and rounded, silver tinted, deep green leaves.

'Cascade Dawn' (*m* x *a*)
D. Heims. The lavender shading on the brownish/greyish leaves is consistent all season and it makes a good foliage plant being a sibling of 'Pewter Veil'. The flowers are cream and 40cm (16in) high in June and July.

'Cathedral Windows' (*m* x *a*)
D. Heims, 1996. A good foliage plant with full dark leaves showing patches of purple between dark grey veins.

'Champagne Bubbles'
D. Heims. (PP & EU) Masses of small, white flowers fade rose-red on 55cm (22in) stems – a compact plant with glossy foliage.

Charles Bloom ('Chablo') (*briz*)
A. Bloom, 1993. This was selected and named for Alan Bloom's father. The soft pink, arching sprays of flowers 40cm (16in) high in May and July rise above green leaves.

'Chartreuse' (*cyl*)
Light green flowers contrast with purple leaves.

'Chatterbox' (*s*)
The leaves are the typical *sanguinea* and make a compact plant good for edging or ground cover. The rose-pink flowers 30-50cm (12-20in) high are repeat blooming particularly in cooler areas. Will grow in sun or partial shade.

'Checkers'
C. Oliver. This has cream flowers 40cm (16in) high, over silver foliage, in June and July.

'Cherries Jubilee'
D. Heims. (PP & EU) Cherry coloured flowers 45cm (18in) high appear from April until August above warm, brown, ruffled foliage that is veiled in shadier locations.

'Cherry Splash' (*briz*)(v)
White and gold splashes on green foliage, more pronounced in spring, with cherry-red flowers 45cm (18in) high in late spring. Similar to 'Splish Splash'.

'Chiqui' (*cyl* x *s*)
A George Schenk hybrid. The single, salmon pink flowers are the largest of all in this genus and are borne on spiky clusters 45cm (18in) high. The leaves are a vivid light green, compact, and slightly hairy.

'Chocolate Ruffles' (*m* x *a*)
D. Heims, 1995. (PP & EU). The matt, deeply cut, very ruffled leaves are chocolate on top and burgundy on the underside. The small flowers grow 75cm high in purple spikes. A very attractive hybrid that has won several awards.

'Chocolate Veil' AGM (*m* x *a*)
D. Heims. This tough hybrid has almost black, smooth leaves with purple highlights and pink/cream flowers. Grows up to 25cm (10in) across and 30cm (1ft) tall.

'Chocolate White'
Grown for its foliage of white and brown; the flower stems are 40cm (16in) high in June and July.

'Cinde' (*v*)
This is one of the shorter cultivars and has red flowers to 35cm (14in) high, from May to July, over white and green variegated foliage.

'City Lights'
D. Heims, 2004. (PPAF & PPR). A bronze leaved, vigorous hybrid with luminous, cream coloured flowers over chocolate leaves. It is very floriferous.

'Claudia'
Another shorter cultivar with pink flowers 35cm (14in) high, in June and July, over green leaves.

'Constance' (*r* x *v*)
Blooming in June and July the flowers are coral pink, 35cm (14in) tall, and the leaves are green.

'Coral Bouquet'
C. Oliver, 1997. A hybrid from *H. cylindrica* x *H.* x *brizoides*. The green leaves have some silver patterning and a yellow edge to them. The flowers are large, shining pink. It thrives best in full sun with good drainage. A good plant.

'Coral Cloud' (*briz*)
A. Bloom, 1932. Many small, bright coral-pink flowers, 75cm (30in) high, are borne on large wide panicles in May and June, contrasting with silvery leaves.

'Corallion' (*s*)
A. Bloom, 1932. This was outstanding at the time of introduction having large, coral-rose flowers 50-60cm (20-24in) tall. Sadly, it is now probably extinct.

'Cramoisi' (*s*)
This has the typical leaves of the species but very rich coloured red flowers.

'Crimson Cascade'
A. Bloom, 1932. Similar to 'Coral Cloud' but the flowers are a deeper red colour.

'Crimson Cloud' (*briz*)
Green leaves with silver veins and crimson flowers.

'Crimson Curls'
Ray Brown. (PP). Happy in light shade and part sun, this plant has the heaviest ruffled foliage of dark burgundy red with undersides of purple. It forms a 45cm (18in) wide clump and the foliage is persistent in the winter.

'Crispy Curly'
Very convoluted parsley-like foliage with sprays of greenish-white flowers up to 60cm (2ft) high.

'Crown Jewel'
Grown for the beautiful leaves that are green, grey and silver with good venation and maroon undersides.

'Cultus Bay Beauty' (*briz*)
Pink flowers and purple veined leaves.

'Dainty Bells' (*H. hirsutissima*)
Dara Emery 1989 Santa Barbara Botanical Garden. A compact, low growing plant with good rosy pink flowers 20cm (8in) high from April until June. Needs protection from afternoon sun.

Dale's Strain
D. Hendricks. This is a seed propagated strain of *H. americana* from eastern USA selected for the showy foliage. The leaves are boldly marked with silver and in the autumn variable amounts of maroon veining appear, followed by autumn colours in the cooler weather. The small, greenish flowers appear in spring and grow 75cm (2½ft) high. A very tough plant that does well on difficult rocky banks in dry, light shade.
This is not to be confused with *H. americana* **'Mrs Dale'**, an old reddish-leaved cultivar grown for many years in the Red Borders at

Hidcote and nothing at all to do with Dale Hendricks.

'Damask' (*briz*)
Elegant sprays of rich carmine-pink flowers grow to 50cm (20in).

'Dappled Barbara' (v)
This has cream, speckled pinwheel leaves.

'Dark Beauty' (Known as 'Black Beauty' in USA)
D. Heims. (PP & EU). This has pink flowers 40cm (16in) high, in May and June, above glossy, ruffled leaves of dull, ruby red.

'Dark Delight' see 'Martha's Compact'

'David'
Selected by Mary Ramsdale and named for her son. The creamy-rose coloured flowers are 40cm (16in) high and bloom from May until June and the leaves are bronze. Recommended.

'Denis Davison' (*briz*)
The leaves have dark bronze leaf veins and pale sage green highlights. The salmon coloured bells appear in summer, growing to 45cm (18in). It is similar to *H.* 'Huntsman'.

'Diana Clare'
Blooms a little later, from June until September. The flowers are 40cm (16in) high and rose coloured, complementing the brown and red foliage.

'Dingle Amber' (*H. m.* var. *d.*)
M. Handley. Probably from 'Palace Purple', as it has similar characteristics and was a chance seedling. It has a definite orangey-brown cast to the leaf and creamy-white flowers.

'Dingle Mint Chocolate' (*H. m.* var. *d.*)
M. Handley. This is also a chance seedling from 'Palace Purple'. It is evergreen and has large chocolate-brown leaves, edged lime green in the spring but fading in the summer. It has cream flowers in summer like its parent, growing to 60cm (2ft).

Ebony and Ivory = E and I (**'Ebony and Ivory'** is the statutory name in USA)
D. Heims. (PP & EU). Large ivory flowers for a long period from April onwards are held 45cm (18in) high over ruffled, ebony coloured leaves. A very showy and distinctive plant.

'Eco-improved' (*m* x *a*)
D. Jacobs. This has all the characteristics of 'Eco-magnififolia' but smoother, larger leaves show an improved contrast and are a brighter silver.

'Eco-magnififolia' (*m* x *a*)
D. Jacobs. This is said to be *H. americana* subsp. *heteradenia*. It is a semi-evergreen, with dark grey, tri-lobed leaves edged with silver and having purple veins. The flowers are of the *H. micrantha* type. It is very tolerant of heat and humidity.

'Eden's Aurora'
The flowers are yellow and rise 60cm (2ft) over green leaves in May and June.

'Eden's Joy'
The pink flowers rise 25cm (10in) above shiny, green leaves and will re-bloom later in the summer.

'Eden's Mystery'
The dark, shiny, purple leaves become a glossy silver later and the creamy-white flowers are 25cm (10in) high.

'Eden's Shine'
Very showy spikes of bright red flowers 50cm (20in) high rise above shiny, dark green leaves in June.

'Edge Hall' (*briz*)
A good, pink flowered hybrid. The rather bunched flower heads suggest *H. cylindrica* in its breeding.

'Elvira'
Scalloped edged leaves and many pink flowers that are good for cutting.

'Emerald Veil' (*m* x *a*)
The 1m (39in) tall flowers in June and July are cream coloured and the foliage is green and silver.

'Emperor's Cloak'
A stunning variety with puckered, folded and pleated leaves from beetroot red to deep purple. Fluffy, white flowers contrast well, rising to 45cm (18in) high.

'Emperor's New Clothes'
K. Sahin, 2002. A seed-raised cultivar. Wonderful foliage plants that provide an assortment of colours and leaf forms over the season. Fantastic border, edging and container specimens. Sun or partial shade. Height to 60cm (2ft).

'Fackel' (*s*)
Dark red flowers and good bronze foliage.

'Fairy Cups' (*briz*)
Distinctive dark, cherry-red cupped flowers and good foliage.

'Feuerlohe' (*s*)

The 40cm (16in) red flowers appear in May and June, above typical *sanguinea* foliage.

Feuerregen see 'Pluie de Feu' (Rain of Fire)

'Firebird' (*briz*)

A. Bloom, 1950. A very good, erect, compact, plant bearing many intense deep red flowers 60cm (2ft) high.

Firefly see 'Leuchtkäfer')

'Fire Sprite' (*briz*)

Rose red flowers.

'Fireworks' AGM

D. Heims. (PP & EU) The matt green leaves have deeply frilled edges that expose the wine-red reverse. The 20cm (8in) high, coral pink flowers appear in early summer making this an attractive compact plant that enjoys partial shade. This is a sibling of Ebony and Ivory.

'Florist's Choice'

D. Heims. (PP & PVR). Huge flowering stems of rich red blooms rise almost 1m (39in) high. A good cut flower that prefers full sun but will perform in half shade.

'Freedom' (*s*)

A. Bloom, 1932. This has large rose-pink flowers on compact sprays to 50cm (20in). The leaves are marbled light green.

'Frosted Violet'

C. Oliver, 2002. (PPAF). This new introduction has the vigour and habit of other *H. villosa* types. The new leaves are a pink-violet that in winter turns bluish-violet. The flowers are like pink, seed pearls, 70cms (28in) high, and appear from late spring until late summer.

'Frosty' (*s*) (*v*)

D. Heims. Bright splashed variegated foliage contrasts well with the deep red flowers growing to 50cm (20in).

'Gaiety' (*s*) A. Bloom, 1932. The many, 50cm (20in) high, large flowers of carmine-rose pink flowers appear in May and June and the foliage is green. It is a little taller than 'Freedom'.

'Garnet' (*m* x *a*)

R. Lightly, 1989. This chance seedling has yellowish-green flowers 30-75cm (12-30in) high. The emerging leaves are purplish changing to green with bronzed veins all summer, and then reverting to an intense garnet centre with a green margin in cold winter weather.

'Geisha's Fan' (*s*)
D. Heims. (PPAF). The dark-veiled leaves darken as they age and become fan-shaped. A good plant with pink flowers 40cm (16in) high in May and June.

'Genevieve' (*s* x *max*)
Rancho Santa Ana Botanic Garden. Lee Lenz, 1974. Rose pink flowers growing up to 60cm (2ft) high from spring until late summer. Light green marbled foliage

'Gloriana' (*s*)
A. Bloom, 1950. The flowers are a bright, deep pink, 60cm (2ft) high. The name was eventually dropped in favour of 'Carmen'. (A mistake in naming meant that it had also been known as 'Captivation' though it is not quite the same. 'Captivation' was dropped as too much like 'Gloria'.)

'Gold Dust' (*s*)
Chartreuse-coloured foliage.

'Gracillima' (*briz*)
Wallace 1902. A very old hybrid having slender, pink panicles of small flowers 50cm (20in) high in early summer.

'Grandiflora' (*s*)
A vigorous plant with large, crimson to scarlet flowers 45cm (18in) high.

'Greenfinch' (*cyl*)
This is a green-flowered selection. The true plant is a bold, strong grower, with silver-marbled leaves and stiff, upright stems 90cm (3ft) high, blooming from spring to midsummer. Most plants in the trade do not resemble the original and are likely to be seedlings.

'Green Ivory' (*cyl*)
A. Bloom, 1968. The green blooms, 75cm (2½ft) high from spring to midsummer, delight the flower arranger. It will not tolerate drought, and is a seedling of 'Greenfinch'.

'Green Light'
The 40cm (16in) high, white flowers appear in May and June and the leaves are green.

'Green Marble' (*cyl*)
A. Bloom, 1973. The greenish white flowers are accompanied by light green marbled foliage.

'Green Spice' (*a*)
D. Heims. The bright green, scalloped leaves are overlaid with silver and the dark veins turn orange and purple in autumn when the leaves

are edged a darker green. Whitish green flowers appear in spring.

'Gypsy Dancer'
D. Heims, 2004. This is similar to 'Can-can' with a multitude of light pink flowers accompanied by dark, veiled foliage. A repeat flowerer, it enjoys part shade to full sun and stays small.

'Harmonic Convergence'
C. Oliver, 1997 (PP) (A Bloom's selection). The bold patterned bronze and silver foliage supports 45cm (18in) loose spikes of frilly, pink, bell-like flowers over a long period in late spring and summer.

'Harry Hay' (*a*)
This plant is similar to 'Chocolate Ruffles' but the leaves are more palmate in shape.

'Hearts on Fire'
C. Oliver, 2003. (PPAF). This has won awards in the USA. Beautiful ruffled red and silver foliage and pure white flowers 60cm (2ft) high.

'Helen Dillon' (v)
Has pretty cream-speckled and splashed leaves that become greener in the winter. A vigorous and good plant with red flowers 50cm (20in) high from May until July. Needs good conditions to do well – loamy and moist soil.

'Hercules' (v)
EU. The cream and green marbled foliage gives rise to dark red flowers. This is similar to 'Monet' but larger.

'Heuros'
A. Bloom. (PP. PVR in UK only). In the USA this is known as 'Rosemary Bloom', named for Adrian Bloom's wife. It has coral pink flowers 40-60cm (16-24in) high in early summer and rich green foliage.

'High Society'
The pewter coloured leaves have charcoal veins and the large flowers are ivory, 40cm (16in) high. It is long blooming from April until June and later.

'Hob' (*pub*)
The winter leaves are a dull, glowing orange-red. It looks good with orange primroses. The white flowers appear in April until June and rise to 45cm (18in). An easy plant.

'Huntsman' (*briz*)
Clear, bright salmon pink flowers grow to 50cm (20in) from late spring to midsummer, but it is not very free flowering. The leaves are mid-green.

'Hyperion' (*cyl*)
A. Bloom, 1959. Short stemmed and very free flowering with soft rosy red flowers with a hint of green. The leaves are marbled. A compact plant.

'Ibis' (*s*)
A. Bloom, 1950. Sturdy sprays of deep pink blooms appear from spring to late summer. Originally described as excellent for the front of the border because of its long flowering period.

'Jack Frost' (*s*)
The rose coloured flowers complement the very silvery foliage.

'Jade Gloss'
C. Oliver, 2001. (PP) Best in sun or part shade, this makes a small, compact clump of slightly cupped, stunning silver foliage with dramatic dark purple veining. It is heavy flowering with 45cm (18in) tall stems in spring, bearing pink buds that open to white.

JCA 9508
Introduced by J. Archibald. The pink flowers only rise to 12cm (5in) over neat, red tinted foliage.

'Jubilee' (*s*)
A. Bloom. 1932. This was named for the Silver Jubilee of George V. The pink flowers are paler than 'Edge Hall' growing to 50cm (25in) in early summer. A compact and reliable plant.

JLS 86275 CLOR (*H. m.* var *d.*)
J. Sharman. The seed was collected in Oregon, USA. The individually tiny, white flowers are borne on long brush-like spikes 60cm (2ft) high. It is good for a moist, shady bank but will grow in most conditions. The leaves are green with grey or purple markings and it is one of the few heucheras to run and form a carpet or ground cover.

'June Bride' (*briz*)
Has white, pink tinted flowers and originated from a batch of seedlings raised as Bressingham hybrids.

'Jupiter'
Flowers are 40cm (16in) high in May and June.

'Just So'
White flowers 50cm (20in) high in May and June over green leaves.

'Khaki Sheds' (*m*)
The strange, apricot sectorial variegations on brown leaves make this a plant for the enthusiast. They are accompanied by open sprays of small, dull brown flowers 55cm (22in) high in May and June.

'Krinkle'
White flowers 40cm (16in) high in June and July rise above green leaves.

'Lace Ruffles'
The flowers are taller at 1m (39in) and cream, in May and June, with green foliage.

'Lady in Red'
Leaves are a reddish-purple with a silver overlay and the red flowers rise to 30cm (1ft) in June and July.

'Lady Romney' (*briz*) (v)
A. Bloom, 1950. The small flowered, soft pink, open panicles bloom 60cm (2ft) high, and are accompanied by marbled leaves.

Larenim hybrids
C. Oliver. A selection of crosses between particularly showy individuals of *H. pubescens* and *H. brizoides* with relatively large pink flowers up to 45cm (18in).

'Larenim Queen'
C. Oliver, 1997. Large, vigorous selection from *H. pubescens* x *H. sanguinea*. The green leaves have a hint of grey marbling, and the sprays of quite large flowers 60-70cm (24-28in) are pink. It is similar to 'Wendy' but very hardy.

'Leuchtkäfer' (*briz*) (Firefly, Glow Worm)
This true-breeding seed raised cultivar has large panicles of vermilion-red, fragrant flowers, 40cm (16in) high that are good for cutting. The green leaves are hairy.

'Lillian's Pink' (*H. pilosissima* x *H.s.*)
A Ron Lutsko selection from California Flora Nursery. The pale pink flowers in spring and summer rise from persistent green leaves. Prefers cool sunny conditions.

'Lime Rickey'
D. Heims, 2004. The exotic leaf colour is a frosted and ruffled lime green with chartreuse leaves in spring. Bearing small, pure white flowers, it is vigorous and looks good in containers.

'Little Dark Girl'
The pink flowers rise above brown foliage 30cm (1ft) high from May to July. An attractive combination.

'Magic Wand' AGM
D. Heims. (PP & EU). The brilliant, cerise/magenta red flowers up to

30cm (1ft) high are a distinct improvement on 'Raspberry Regal' and it will re-bloom in good conditions. The glossy green foliage is clump forming.

'Mardi Gras'
D. Heims. Grown for the huge leaves that range in colour from coral to orange and shades of green through to grey. Every plant is different and will grow in sun or shade.

'Marielle'
Pink flowers 70cm (28in) high appear in June and July, and the leaves are green.

'Margarita'
The 40cm (16in) high pink flowers appear in May and June, and the foliage is brown.

'Marmalade'
D. Heims, 2004. The rich, shining, undulating foliage ranges in colour from umber to a deep sienna. It stands well in inclement weather and bears red/brown flowers.

'Mars'
The pale purple-red foliage is patterned with dark veins and the flowers appear on 30cm (1ft) stems from May until July.

'Martha's Compact' (*m*)
Delicate sprays of small, white flowers 20cm (8in) high, appear from April until June. The lobed leaves are dark and hairy.

'Martha Roderick' (*m*)
Mrs. Roderick's selection from Weott, named by Nevin Smith. This has big, billowing masses of small, pink flowers, 40cm (16in) high, from April until July. A good, robust plant.

'Mary Rose' (*s*)
A. Bloom, 1932. The large, clear, deep pink flowers are erect and 50cm (20in) high.

'Matin Bells' (*briz*)
Coral red flowers.

'Mayfair'
This is a cross between *H.* x *brizoides* and *H. hallii*. It is distinguished by small leaves and pink bells. 30cm (1ft) high.

'Mercury'
The mint-green foliage has scalloped edges and black marbling and the flowers rise to 30cm (1ft) from May until July.

'Midnight Burgundy'
C. Oliver, 2003. An improved form of 'Midnight Claret' with cream flowers and larger purple leaves with extensive silvering. Vigorous and good.

'Midnight Claret'
C. Oliver, 1998. This has probably the darkest purple leaves of any heuchera. They are marked with small patches of light grey and it bears creamy-greenish flowers.

'Mini Mouse'
The pale pink flowers rise above burgundy-coloured leaves.

'Mint Frost'
D. Heims. (EU). The large, frosted, green leaves have red markings and turn pinkish in winter. The pink flowers are 25cm (10in) high.

'Mint Julep' (*m* x *a*)
D. Heims, 1996. This is a shimmering plant with the brightest silver overlay on the mint-green leaves. A good foliage plant.

'Molly Bush' AGM (*m*)
Named for the daughter of Allen Bush, manager of North American branch of Jellito Seeds. In May and June, cream flowers rise 40cm (16in) high, contrasting with brownish/purple foliage. With more consistent darker foliage it performed better at the RHS trials than 'Palace Purple'.

'Monet' (*s*) (*v*)
D. Heims. The dark red flowers rise 38cm (15in) high in May and June, from green and cream marbled foliage that turns pink in the autumn.

'Montrose Ruby'
C. Oliver. The result of a cross between *H. micrantha* 'Palace Purple' x *H. americana* Dale's strain. Bronzed, burgundy-red leaves marked with patches of silver grey give rise to a glowing red in cold weather. The small white flowers appear in late spring onwards on 60cm (2ft) stems. A good, vigorous plant, this is involved in many of the new introductions.

'Moondrops' (*cyl*)
A. Bloom. The leaves are mid-green and slightly silvered. The flowers are a very pale cream with tips tending to pink about 45cm (18in) high.

'Mother of Pearl' (*briz*)
Green and pink flowers grow to 45cm (18in). The dark green leaves are bold and pretty.

'Mount Saint Helen's
Brick red flowers 40cm (16in) high appear in May and June above green foliage.

'Mrs Dale'
An old, reddish leaved cultivar that was for many years grown in the red Border at Hidcote.

'Nancy'
The foliage is brown and the flowers appear in June and July and are 60cm (2ft) high.

'Neptune'
The leaves are pewter-purple with very dark veins and the flowers appear from May until July and are 30cm (1ft) high. The deep division of the leaves imparts a lively appearance to the plant.

'Northern Fire' (s)
The dark green leaves have a silvery sheen under bold spikes of bright red flowers 50cm (20in) high in May and June. Tight habit.

'Oakington Jewel' (s)
A. Bloom, 1932. Named after Alan Bloom's nursery at Oakington, near Cambridge, its fairly large flowers are crimson in colour and grow to 60cm (2ft). The leaves are dark green with a hint of metallic purple and strong veining. In spring, the new leaves rising from the centre of the plant are a rich rosy red.

'Obsidian' Good
D. Heims. (PVR). The really black leaves are round, smooth, shiny and broad and the flowers are yellow. Will grow in sun or partial shade.

'Old la Rochette' (s x max)
Victor Reiter, 1950s. This has an abundance of large, soft pink flowers 60-90cm (2-3ft) high over a mound of large, deep, fuzzy, olive green foliage. Good plant.

'Opal' (s. x max).
Rancho Santa Ana Botanic Garden. Lee Lenz. Very large green foliage and white flowers that age to pink 60cm (2ft) high from May until June. This is durable, robust and easy; long-lived but not sun tolerant.

'Orphée' (briz)
White flowers.

'Painted Lady' (m)
Nevin Smith introduction. The very pretty, sparkling pink and white flowers on dark, pink stems rise in May and June, 55cm (22in) above crinkled, green leaves marked with pewter and red. A good plant that needs light, well-drained soil and light dappled shade.

Heuchera 'Persian Carpet'

'Palace Passion'
D. Heims This hybrid involves *HH. americana, sanguinea,* and 'Palace Purple'. It is more sun resistant than the latter and was the first to combine the chocolate/purple leaves with silver overlay with rose-pink flowers.

'Palace Purple' (*H.m.* var. *d.*)
Introduced by B. Halliwell, this colourful variety has very strong blackish-purple leaves, sometimes with a metallic sheen. The tiny, white flowers are borne above the foliage. Americans, apparently, are bemused by the popularity of this plant in the UK as in parts of the USA it is considered a weed. It was originally given an AGM but this has since been withdrawn because it has often been produced from seed but does not come absolutely true.

'Palace Purple Select' (*H.m.* var. *d.*)
This is a true-breeding seed-raised purplish-leaved variety from Jellito.

'Patricia Louise'
A good plant for shade with large, soft pink bells on tall stems. It is excellent for cutting.

'Pearl Drops' (*briz*)
A. Bloom, 1950. As the name suggests the small flowers are an opalescent white with a hint of pink. They are borne on arching sprays 60cm (2ft) high.

'Pearl Pendants'
C. Oliver 1999. The bronze leaves have light silver markings and the pale pink flowers are large and showy on 60cm (2ft) stems. It is exceptionally vigorous.

'Persian Carpet' (*m x a*)
D. Heims. The flat leaves are up to 20cm (8in) wide and have metallic shadings on dark red with purple veins and edging. An excellent winter foliage plant with *H. micrantha* type flowers.

The 'Petite' Series all hail from Charles Oliver's nursery 'Primrose Path' and, as would be expected, are 'miniatures'.

'Petite Bronze Pearl'
1997. The flowers are cream over brown foliage in May and June and are 30cm (1ft) high.

'Petite Lime Sherbet'
1997. Small, green leaves with bold silver veins support bright pink flowers 30cm (1ft) high.

'Petite Marbled Burgundy'
(PP) 1997. Bronze leaves with strong silver markings and light, pink flowers 30cm (1ft) high.

'Petite Pearl Fairy'
(PP) 1997. This has small, bronze leaves marbled silver and medium pink flowers up to 25cm (10in). It requires rich soil and full sun and is very floriferous.

'Petite Pink Bouquet'
1997. The green leaves have a reddish tinge and light silver misting and the large, medium-pink flowers grow up to 20cm (8in). It makes a small, neat plant.

'Petite Ruby Frills'
1998. Bronze leaves, silver markings, and pink flowers up to 30cm (1ft) form a clump intermediate between 'Pearl Fairy' and 'Marbled Burgundy'.

'Pewter Moon' (briz)
P. Oudolf. This has pewter-marbled, scalloped foliage with maroon colour on the reverse. The ice-pink flowers reach 30cm (1ft) from May until July and the leaves are very good in winter.

'Pewter Veil' (m x a)
D. Heims. (PP & EU) The copper/pink spring foliage of this semi-evergreen turns pewter-purple with age. The leaves are up to 15cm (6in) wide, with silver netting between the veins.

'Pink Cloud' (briz)
Pink flowers.

'Pink Lipstick'
D. Heims, 2004. (PPAF & PVR) Columnar spikes of pink flowers rise above vigorous green foliage that takes on red overtones in winter. It is low growing.

'Pink Love'
Pink flowers 30cm (1ft) high in May and June coupled with green foliage.

'Pink Ruffles'
Pinkish/brown ruffled foliage contrasts with cream flowers 50cm (20in) high in May and June.

'Pink Spray'
A. Bloom, 1930. The pink flowers are fewer in number than in some of Alan Bloom's other cultivars.

'Pink Wave' (*eleg* x *s*)
Santa Barbara Botanic Garden 1991. Good rosettes of leaves form tight mats of green leaves with 30cm (1ft) high panicles of sparkling rosy pink and white flowers. Needs protection from afternoon sun.

'Pluie de Feu' (Feuerregen) (*briz*)
Good persistent, glowing red panicles are borne 40cm (16in) high in midsummer over green leaves.

'Plum Pudding'
D. Heims, 1996. (EU). This has shimmering, plum-purple, shiny foliage and a tight habit, making a good foil for the variegated forms. Very popular.

'Pretty Polly' (*briz*)
A. Bloom, 1950. This has a dwarf habit, 30cm (1ft) tall, and very large, free-flowering, clear rose pink flowers.

'Primrose Path' (*mer*)
C. Oliver. A tidy plant with lemony-cream flowers over darkish green leaves. Growing only 15cm (6in) high, it is mat forming.

'Prince'
This dramatic plant has dark purple-red leaves with ruffled edges and 50cm (20in) high purple stems of white flowers emerging from lime green calyces from May until June.

'Prince of Orange'
Foliage of orange/brown is accompanied by cream flowers 35cm (14in) high in May and June.

'Prince of Silver'
PVR. The silvery foliage contrasts with the pink flowers 35cm (14in) high in May and June – recommended.

'Purple Mountain Majesty'
C. Oliver. Compact purple foliage with light silver pattern and very large globular white flowers, 45-50cm (18-20in) in spring. More sun tolerant than most heucheras.

'Purple Petticoats' AGM
D. Heims, 1996. (EU) A good, tough, foliage plant with dark, congested leaves that have purple highlights and burgundy on the underside. Similar to 'Stormy Seas' but with more intensely ruffled leaves. Flowers are cream coloured. Recommended.

'Purple Sails' (*m* x *a*)
D. Heims, 1996. A hybrid of *H. micrantha* and *H. americana*, the leaves are very dark purple and upright and have a metallic sheen, growing to 10cm (4in) across. When mature they spiral into a helix.

'Quick Silver'
The dark smokey leaves with purple veining are accompanied by white flowers.

X 'Quilter's Joy' AGM
C. Oliver, 1997. The purple leaves turn silvery-purple and the 45cm (18in) high creamy-pink flowers appear in June and July.

'Rachel' (*briz*)
M. Ramsdale, 1989 and named for her granddaughter. A good plant with interest all year. It is a cross between *H*. 'Sunset' and *H*. 'Palace Purple'. The purple-flushed, dull green-grey leaves have maroon undersides and the red stems bear many small flowers that look like pale pink foam. It blooms for months from spring through to midsummer. 30cm (1ft) high.

'Red Prince'
Very, very floriferous. Brilliant scarlet flowers from June to mid-August. Green leaves.

'Rainbow'
Grown for the leaves that are randomly blotched with colours of dark and pale green with a pink and red wash.

'Raspberry Ice'
C. Oliver, 2002. (PP) Happy in sun or partial shade this is a sister seedling to the same breeder's 'Silver Scrolls'. It has lovely silver foliage with dark purple veins and a dark purple overlay. Each vigorous 60cm (2ft) clump is topped in late spring with 60cm (2ft) tall spikes of large pink flowers.

X 'Raspberry Regal' AGM
This appears to be a hybrid between *H. cylindrica* and *H.* x *brizoides* It has raspberry-red, poker-like spikes of flowers on dark stems and green leaves overlaid with silver. The flowers, which appear from May to July are up to 60cm (2ft) high.

'Raspberry Sorbet'
The raspberry-red double sized flowers are borne on a wand-shaped stem. It is a repeat bloomer and it is good for cutting.

'Red Arrow'
Green foliage combines with red flowers 40cm (16in) high in May and June.

'Red Bird'
Originated in Holland but quickly became obsolete. It has rather rounded, scallop shaped, light purple-red leaves much lighter in colour

than all the other chocolate coloured cultivars. Palest ivory pink flowers appear in June and July and grow 50cm (20in) high.

'Red Bud' (*cyl*)
Introduced by Siskiyou Rare Plant Nursery. Red buds open to creamy flowers.

'Red Pimpernel' (*briz*)
A vigorous plant bearing 50-60cm (20-24in) high flowers of a scarlet to coral colour with green leaves.

'Red Spangles' (*briz*) AGM
A. Bloom, 1950. The large bright scarlet flowers bloom in the spring and again in late summer on stems 40-60cm (16-24in) tall with abundant foliage.

'Regal Robe' (*m* x *a*)
D. Heims, 1998. A compact plant with very large silver/lavender marbled leaves. Evergreen and a good specimen plant.

'Regina' AGM
C. Oliver, 1997. The leaves are a medium-red purple colour with silver between the veins. The large, strong pink flowers on 90cm (3ft) stems bloom over a long period from April until August. An excellent plant.

'Rhapsody' (*briz*) A. Bloom. 1967. The raiser considered that this had the best pink flowers at the time.

'Ridges'
Green leaves with white flowers 40cm (16in) high in May and June.

'Ring of Fire' (*a*)
D. Heims. A seedling of 'Eco-magnififolia', it is a silver leaved plant suffused with purple along the veins. In autumn the leaves are rimmed a bright coral colour.

'Robusta' (s)
Typical *sanguinea* but the flowers are much larger and a darker red.

'Rocket' (Rakete) (*briz*)
From early summer onwards, bright vermilion flowers rise 60-70cm (24- 28in) over dark green leaves.

'Rondi'
Red flowers 40cm (16in) high in May and June, with green leaves.

'Ronstar'
Pink flowers 40cm (16in) high in May and June with brownish leaves.

'Rosada' (*max* x *s*)
A good selection from the University of California at Davis, probably a Don Sexton hybrid that had been in the Arboretum for over 30 years

before being named. The evergreen foliage is similar to 'Wendy' but the soft pink and white flowers are smaller and borne in more open and delicate panicles. Prefers cool, sunny conditions. Good landscape use of this plant was made at The Santa Ana Botanic Garden.

'Rosea' (*s*)
Rose coloured flowers about 45cm (18in) high.

'Rosemary Bloom' see 'Heuros'

'Rose Mirrors'
C. Oliver, 2002. (PP). The medium pink, showy flowers rise 45cm (18in) above dark purple and silver foliage.

'Royal Velvet'
C. Oliver. Leaves are rich, dark purple and silver, slightly pubescent, ruffled and frilled. Abundant white flowers in spring. 45cm (18in). Unusual.

'Ruby Mist'
This is a good spring and summer performer with reddish flowers from late February until June. Very floriferous, with mid-green foliage.

'Ruby Bells' (*s*)
A true-breeding seed-raised cultivar. Very floriferous; intense blood-red flowers to 40cm (16in). Fragrant. Green foliage.

'Ruby Ruffles' (*m* x *a*)
D. Heims. This is a cross between 'Ruffles' and 'Pewter Veil' being more ruffled and having a silver metallic overlay to the ruby leaves.

'Ruby Veil' (*m* x *a*)
D. Heims. The leaves, 20cm (8in) across, have metallic slate-grey venation over velvety, ruby-red foliage. This is very sun tolerant and reliable.

'Ruffles' (*m*)
Ruffled ridges on the woolly leaves form an attractive mound. The small, white flowers grow to 60cm (2ft).

SanPico hybrids (*H. pulchella* x *H. hallii*)
C. Oliver. These plants form low mounds of small leaves with light pink bell flowers in spring on dark coloured stems 20-25cm (8-10 in) high.

'SanPico Rosita'
C. Oliver, 1995. The short-stemmed cream flowers bloom over a long period from May to August and the leaves are green.

'Santa Ana Cardinal' (*s* x *max*)
Lee Lenz, 1958, Rancho Santa Ana Botanic Garden. A robust plant with dark shiny green foliage and scarlet/red flowers up to 90cm (3ft) high.

'Santa Rosa'
Pink flowers 25cm (10in) high appear in May and June; the leaves are green.

'Sashay' AGM
D. Heims. A sport from 'Purple Petticoats'. It has contrasting bi-coloured leaves, dark green on top and burgundy on the reverse and ruffled. The flowers are 50cm (20 in) high and good for cutting

'Saturn'
Very rounded leaves have dark veining over a pewter background and narrow reddish edges. The flowers appear from May to July on 30cm (1ft) stems.

'Saturnale'
Red flowers 35cm (14in) high in May and June with green leaves.

'Schneewittchen' (Snow White) (*briz*)(v)
The white flowers rise above light green, variegated leaves in summer. It needs good soil and light shade.

'Scintillation' (*briz*) AGM
A. Bloom, 1950. From late spring to early summer this bears 60-70cm (24-28in) high flowers of a vivid pink tipped with carmine. The leaves are marbled with silver. One of Alan Bloom's favourites and a good variety, it has received many RHS awards.

'Shamrock'
D. Heims. The unusual bright green flowers tower 90cm (3ft) over slightly silvered jagged-edged foliage. It blooms from April until September and prefers full sun.

'Shenandoah Mountain'
C. Oliver, 2003. (PPAF). Good, creamy white flowers are held 70cm (28in) high over burgundy and silver foliage. New, and it should be good.

'Shere Variety' (*briz*)
Dainty, brilliant scarlet flower spikes 45cm (18in) high.

'Silberregen' (Silver Rain) (*briz*)
Free flowering with pure white blooms 50cm (20in) high.

'Silky'
Cream flowers 50cm (20in) high in May and June with green leaves.

'Silver Indiana'
(EU). A pretty plant with silver leaves and white flowers 35cm (14in) high in May and June.

'Silver Light'
C. Oliver, 2002. Has the most silvery leaves of all the heucheras, being small and lobed. The upright spikes of frilly, pink flowers appear in late

spring and are 45cm (18in) high. It looks particularly good with cyclamen and the glaucous grasses.

'Silvero'
Silver leaves with pink flowers in May and June on 15cm (6in) stems.

'Silver Lode'
C. Oliver, 2002. (PP) Dark stems bearing pink flowers rise from the green leaves.

'Silver Maps'
C. Oliver, 1999. A seedling from the same batch as 'Silver Lode'.

'Silver Mittens'
From May to June red flowers 30cm (1ft) high rise from mitten-shaped, silver speckled leaves.

'Silver Scrolls'
C. Oliver, 1998. (PP & EU). This outstanding variety has purple veined, silvery leaves with purple on the reverse forming a spiral mound like a stained glass mosaic. Delicate white, upright flowers rise to 60cm (2ft) in early summer.

'Silver Shadows'
D. Heims, 1996. This is very good for the foliage, which is purest dark silver, with a rose overlay in spring. A deep, thick and intense plant with a compact habit and 18cm (8in) leaves.

'Silver Streak'
The leaves are silvered, indented and red. The flowers are 25cm (10in) high in mid summer.

'Silver Veil' (*briz*)
Similar to 'Palace Purple' but the leaf is largely overlaid with silver and the flowers are a cherry-rose colour.

'Silver Veil Improved' (s)
D. Heims. Cerise-rose flowers show well against the netted silver leaves, growing 50cm (20in) high.

'Silvo'
Silver leaves and short stemmed pink flowers in May and June.

'Sioux Falls' (*s* x)
A true-breeding seed strain, this has large, bright red bells, 60-70cm (24-28in) high, in June and July, over deep green foliage. A good plant.

'Smokey Rose' AGM
D. Heims. Browny-pink flowers over foliage the colour of smouldering embers.

'Snow Angel' (*s*) (*v*)
The tall, bright red flowers rise above variegated leaves flecked creamy-white.

'Snowbells' (*glauc*)
This delightful little alpine has rounded, white bells above round, green leaves only 2cm (1in) across.

'Snowdawn'
Ron Lutsko, 1988. A selection of a cross between *H. pilosissima* and *H.* 'Lillian's Pink'

'Snowflakes' (*briz*)
A. Bloom, 1950. A good flowering plant with large, white bells on 50-60cm (20-24in) stems. Needs a sheltered spot for winter protection but is considered by the breeder to be one of the best whites.

'Snow Storm' (*s*) (*v*)
D. Heims. White and green leaves show off the bright cerise flowers growing 45cm (18in) high in the spring. This is a striking plant and will grow in either sun or partial shade. Rumoured to be loved by rabbits!

'Souvenir de Wolley-Dod'
This is an easy plant with sprays of red flowers 60cm (2ft) high in May and June.

'Sparkler' (*briz*) (*v*)
A. Bloom, 1950. Open, light panicles of carmine and scarlet, medium-sized flowers 60cm (2ft) high with variegated leaves. Very free flowering.

'Splendens' (*s*)
The abundant flowers are a bright carmine red.

'Splendour' (*briz*)
A. Bloom, 1953. This has salmon/scarlet flowers 45-60cm (18-24in) high but a poor constitution.

'Splish Splash' (*s*)
D. Heims. Very similar to 'Snow Storm' but the contrast between flowers and leaves is brighter.

'Stormy Seas'
D. Heims, 1995. A striking plant with silver, lavender, pewter and charcoal grey hues on large, heavily ruffled, deeply cut foliage.

'Strawberries and Cream' (*v*)
Cream splashed, ruffled, greyish green leaves and strawberry-pink flowers from May until July, 50cm (20in) high.

'Strawberry Candy'
D. Heims. (PP & EU). Very large, deep pink flowers clustered on tight stems rise 40cm (16in) above marbled, silver-green, ruffled leaves that have an oak leaf shape. It blooms from April until September. Compact, and looks good in containers and stands heat well.

'Strawberry Swirl'
D. Heims, 1995. This looks like a pink bouquet in late spring with up to sixty flower stalks 55cm (22in) high. It is much larger than *sanguinea* and has ruffled fan-like foliage overlaid with silver. Vigorous.

'Sunset' (*briz*)
A. Bloom, 1950. Has large, bright coral-red, late blooming flowers, 50cm (20in) high but is not very vigorous.

'Susannah' (*s x max*)
Lee Lenz, 1974. Named after the founder of the Rancho Santa Ana Botanic Garden, this has very dark pink to red flowers on less branched panicles and dark green, glossy foliage.

'Swirling Fantasy'
(PP & PVR) Another dramatic plant with pewter-red foliage with dark veins supporting 30cm (1ft) high, bright red flowers from May until July.

'Taff's Joy' (*s*)
Very hardy. Bears 35cm (14in) high flowers from spring to midsummer. It was found by HPS member Stephen Taffler in a garden in Chester where it appeared spontaneously in a formal planting of *H. sanguinea*. The leaves are speckled and spotted with creamy-white on a grey background, the margins turning pink in winter. It does best in a shaded position in soil enriched with leaf mould.

'Tall Girl'
The stems grow 70cm (28in) high and bear yellow flowers in May and June over green leaves.

'Tattletale'
The pink flowers grow to 50cm (20in) in May and June above green leaves.

Tinian Bronze'
C. Oliver, 1997. White flowers in May and June over brown leaves.

'Titania' (*briz*)
This is a very old hybrid with vigorous panicles of salmon-pink flowers growing 50-60cm (20-24in) high and is good in exposed positions.

'Torch'
Red flowers from April until May with green foliage.

'Toto'
Red flowers 60cm (2ft) high in May and June with green leaves.

'Trevor Red' (s)
Similar to 'Gracillima' but having larger flowers on shorter stems 45cm (18in) high and of a stronger brilliance.

'True Love'
Tall cream flowers up to 70cm (28in) in May and June over brown leaves.

'Twister'
Cream flowers 40cm (16in) high in May and June with brown leaves.

'Van Gogh'
Cream flowers 50cm (20in) high in May and June, with brown foliage.

'Veil of Passion'
D. Heims. (PP & EU). The fragrant, pink flowers bloom all summer 60cm high (2ft) over dark leaves that have a veiled appearance.

'Velvet Night' (m x a)
One of Dan Heims' darkest cultivars having 20cm (8in) black slate leaves with metallic-purple overlays and deep purple veins. The flowers are 75cm (30in) high. It contrasts well with gold foliage plants. The leaves have a velvety feel.

'Venus'
The large, silver-sheened leaves have dark veining. The flowers, from May until July, are 30cm (1ft) high.

'Vesuvius'
D. Heims. (PP & EU). Profuse orangey-pink flowers rise 60cm (2ft) over purple foliage from April until September. Will grow in sun or partial shade.

'Violet Knight' (m x a)
Good violet coloured leaves with a silvery sheen and deep purple veins.

'Wendy' (max x s)
Santa Ana Botanic Garden. Lee Lenz, 1984. This is outstanding with 90cm (3ft) tall, airy panicles of soft pink blooms accompanied by persistent leaves. Very good in the shady garden. Has the same parentage as 'Opal'.

'Wendy Hardy'
Cream flowers 40cm (16in) high in May and June with green leaves.

'Weserlachs' (briz)
Strong, salmon-pink panicles 60-70cm (24-28in) high appear in May and June.

'White Cloud' (*s*)
Spikes of pure white bells rise to 45cm (18in) in May and June, with pale green leaves overlaid with silver. A seed-raised cultivar.

'White Marble' (*pub. x*)
C. Oliver, 1995. A *H. pubescens* cross, this has huge, white, double-petalled flowers, densely packed on 55cm (22in) stems and silver marbled leaves. It is tolerant of drought.

'White Spires'
D. Heims, 1996. Clouds of tall, airy, white flowers that rise 75cm (18in) high over apple green leaves. It blooms profusely over a long period.

'Whirlwind'
Introduced by D. Heims, 1996. This has fluted and crested foliage that is bronze-green. It has white flowers in April and May and was found in the wild. Vigorous.

'Widar' (*briz*)
A vigorous variety with beautiful, dark scarlet flowers up to 80cm (32in) high.

'Winfield Pink' (s)
Magenta flowers rise above good burgundy-coloured foliage.

'Winter Red'
D. Heims. The spectacular, semi-evergreen, foliage is a rich green with red shading turning all red in the autumn. It flowers from May until June on stems 38cm (15cm) high having showy, fat spikes of large red flowers with small white mouths. It received good reports for its foliage in the RHS trials 1996-98.

'Yeti' (*s*)
Intense green and white leaves support white flowers 20cm (8in) high. Very floriferous.

'Zabeliana'
The greenish-yellow flowers grow to 60cm (2ft) and the leaves are heavily marbled orange-brown when young, later turning green.

X *Heucherella*

THESE ARE INTERGENERIC HYBRIDS between various species of the genera *Heuchera* and *Tiarella*, though the majority are *H. x brizoides* and *Tiarella cordifolia*. They are complex and sometimes difficult to classify accurately. The results of this breeding have given us some of the most beautiful plants for the garden.

Propagation must be by division since these hybrids are sterile. Basal cuttings can be taken in spring or the plants can be divided in the spring or autumn. Surviving in zones 4 -9, all are hardy in the U.K.

x *H. alba*
A soft green, hairy plant with white flowers. Parentage *H. x brizoides* and *Tiarella wherryi*.

x *H.a.* 'Bridget Bloom'
A. Bloom, 1953. Named for his eldest daughter. *Tiarella wherryi* and *Heuchera* 'Freedom' were used in this cross. A charming little plant with soft green, lobed leaves with darker veins clearly marked and elegant sprays of pink-tinged white-petalled flowers 45cm (18in) high. It has a long flowering period from late spring to autumn, preferring light, humus rich soil in partial shade.

x *H.a.* 'Pink Frost'
C. Oliver, 1995. A selected clone, with pink flowers blooming over a long period above lovely frosted foliage. A very popular plant.

x *H.a.* 'Rosalie'
A selection with recurrent, pink flowers to 30cm (1ft) and evergreen, persistent foliage with attractive brown markings.

x *H. a.* 'White Blush'
C. Oliver. The flowers of this selection are white and very pale pink.

x *H.* 'Birthday Cake'
D. Heims, 2004. This forms a chocolate-coloured mound of cut foliage with a topping of creamy, candle-like flowers. A vigorous plant.

x *H.* 'Burnished Bronze'
D. Heims. (PP & PVR). Has large, lacy leaves of shiny, dark chocolate bronze and starry, soft pink flowers 45cm (18in) high in spring.

x *H.* 'Chocolate Lace'
D. Heims. (PP & PVR). Each lacy leaf is milk chocolate coloured and the flowers are 45cm (18in) high and strawberry-pink.

x *H.* 'Cinnamon Bear'
D. Heims. Cinnamon brown foliage with two main leaf tips (looking like ears) is accompanied by tawny, star-like flowers 50cm (20in) high. It will re-bloom during the spring and summer.

x *H.* 'Cranberry Ice'
D. Heims. A delightful, small plant for light shade. The palmate leaves form a dense clump and the dainty flowers are salmon pink tipped with dark cranberry, on pink stems 45cm (18in) high. A good plant for containers it needs protection from hot afternoon sun.

x *H.* 'Dayglow Pink'
D. Heims. (PP & EU). This has branched, brilliant pink flowers 40cm (16in) high, with green leaves that are cut with a chocolate coloured inlay. This is followed in winter by brilliant purple foliage.

x *H.* 'Heart of Darkness'
C. Oliver (PP) 2002. Masses of white foamy flowers on 45cm (18in) stems rise above tri-coloured leaves. These have dark maroon markings on a silver-grey shaded green background. Leaves grown during the cool season are dark maroon with margins of lime green. A spectacular plant.

x *H.* 'Kimono' AGM.
D. Heims. (PP & PVR). Unique kimono-like shaped leaves of silver, purple and green are narrow in spring but grow larger and become huge, round, and palmate in summer. The tawny flowers are 45cm(18in) high and the plant assumes a metallic rose colour in winter.

x *H.* 'Party Time'
D. Heims, 2004. This forms a low clump of green/bronze foliage with a silver overlay. The warm pink flowers bloom over a long period; a good plant.

x *H.* 'Pearl Kohl'
A variegated plant with persistent, maple-shaped leaves of green overlaid with white, forming a clump.

x *H.* 'Pink Frost'
C. Oliver. This very vigorous plant has prominent marbled grey on green foliage and bi-coloured flowers of pink and white.

x *H.* 'Quicksilver'
A Bloom's selection. (PP). Metallic silver foliage with bronze veining. Dark flower stems carry large pale pink blooms fading to white as they open. Vigorous and good, it has a long flowering period from April until June.

x *H.* 'Silver Streak'

D. Heims. 1997. The palm-shaped leaves are overlaid in shades of silver and purple. The profuse, white flowers 50cm (20in) high are tinged with lavender. It is repeat blooming and looks good in winter.

x *H.* 'Snow White'

C. Oliver 1995. White flowers bloom over a mound of apple-green foliage.

x *H.* 'Sunspot'

D. Heims. (PVR). A brilliant new selection of 'Dayglow Pink'. The dramatic yellow leaves have a vivid, blood red patch in their centres. The pink flowers are similar to 'Dayglow Pink' and attain 40cm (16in) in height. The colour fades a little during the summer.

x *H. tiarelloides* AGM

Lemoine, 1917. Round, lobed leaves with scalloped edges give rise to brownish scapes of pink flowers from spring to mid-summer. When planted in patches or drifts they give a light pink, foamy effect. A dainty and pleasing plant. Parentage *H.* x *brizoides* & *Tiarella cordifolia*.

x *H.t.* 'Crimson Clouds'

D. Heims. A selection with double leaves with crimson dots and good pink blooms 40cm (16in) high over a long period.

x *H.* 'Viking Ship'

D. Heims. (PP & EU). The plain, silvered leaf is replaced in summer with a silvered, maple like shape. Coral-pink spires of star-like flowers 45cm (18in) high are branched. Happy in sun or shade this is a good plant.

x *Heucherella* 'Burnished Bronze'

Where to see and buy Heucheras

There is at present one National Collection in the UK belonging to Mrs V. Gilbert. It is open by appointment only and contact should be made to: Mr. B. Russell, Quarry Cottage, Lee, Ilfracombe, Devon EX34 8LR

Many nurseries offer a selection of heucheras for sale; among these are:

Blooms of Bressingham
Bressingham, Diss, Norfolk. IP22 2AB ☎ 01379 688585
www.blooms-online.co.uk

Cotswold Garden Flowers
Brown's Nursery. Gibbs Lane, Offenham, Evesham, Worcs. WR11 8RR
☎ 01386 422829 www.cgf.net

Hardy's Cottage Garden Plants
Freefolk Priors, Freefolk, Whitchurch, Hampshire, RG28 7NJ
☎ 01256 896 533 www.hardys-plants.co.uk

Many gardens open to the public have some of this genus, often in mixed plantings

The following places have collections in the USA:

Rancho Santa Ana Botanic Gardens
1500 North College Avenue, Claremont, California, ☎ 91711-3157
www.rsabg.org

Santa Barbara Botanic Garden
1212 Mission Canyon Road, Santa Barbara, California.
www.santabarbarabotanicgarden.org

Further information may be obtained from :-
The American Association of Botanical Gardens and Arboreta
www.aabga.org
This is a professional association for public gardens in North America.

Other Booklets in the HPS Series

- CAMPANULAS IN THE GARDEN

- EPIMEDIUMS AND OTHER HERBACEOUS BERBERIDACEAE

- EUPHORBIAS

- GRASSES

- HARDY GERANIUMS FOR THE GARDEN

- HOSTAS

- IRISES

- PENSTEMONS

- PHLOX

- PULMONARIAS

- UMBELLIFERS

- SUCCESS WITH SEEDS

Apart from *Success with Seeds*, which is a practical guide to collecting, germinating seed and growing on the resultant plants, each booklet provides comprehensive and practical information on garden-worthy plants in its genus. As well as an invaluable A to Z of species and cultivars, the booklets deal with topics such as cultivation, pests and diseases, propagation, and plant associations. Most booklets include appendices giving information on where to see and where to buy the listed plants. The series has been well received and booklets have attracted excellent reviews.